C000095309

THE HOLDOVERS

A Christmas Comedy movie

David D. Woodcock

DISCLAIMER

This is an analysis of the movie THE HOLDOVERS. It's not a replacement for the movie, and it's not affiliated with the movie industry or the director. The goal of this review is to help people understand the movie.

All rights reserved. No part of this publication may be reproduced, distributed, or transmitted in any form or by any means, including photocopying, recording or other electronic or mechanical methods, without the prior written permission of the publisher, except in the case of brief quotations embodied in critical reviews and certain other non commercial uses permitted by copyright law.

Copyright © David D. Woodcock, 2023

TABLE OF CONTENT

INTRODUCTION

The Handovers is a 2023 American Christmas parody show movie coordinated by Alexander Payne, composed by David Hemingson, and featuring Paul Giamatti, Da'Vine Bliss Randolph and Dominic Sessa. Set in 1970, it follows a pugnacious history educator at Another Britain life experience school who is compelled to chaperone the small bunch of understudies with no place to go over Christmas break.

The film debuted at the 50th Telluride Film Celebration on August 31, 2023, and was delivered in the US, by Center Highlights, on October 27, 2023. It got positive surveys from pundits and has earned $17 million. It was named one of the main 10 movies of 2023 by the Public Leading group of Audit and the American Film Foundation and has gotten numerous different honors, including three designations at the 81st Brilliant Globe Grants.

PLOT

Paul Hunham is a strict, hidebound classics professor at Barton Academy, the New England boarding school that he once attended. He is loathed by his understudies, for his cruel reviewing and harsh demeanor, as well as his kindred staff, because of costing the faculty a significant contributor, in the wake of failing the benefactor's child in his group.

Hunham is compelled to manage the "holdover" students left on campus for the holidays, including Angus Tully, whose mother has unexpectedly arranged a wedding trip with his new stepfather. Likewise remaining behind is cafeteria executive Mary Sheep, who is lamenting the death of her child, a Barton former student killed serving in the Vietnam War.

Hunham forces examining and practicing on the remnants' break, unfortunately. Following six days, a handover's rich dad shows up, by helicopter, and consents to take every one of the understudies on the family's ski trip. Angus can't arrive at his folks for authorization, letting him be at Barton with Hunham and Mary.

Hunham discovers him requiring lodging, prompting a pursuit around the school, until Angus rebelliously jumps into a heap of gym equipment, dislocating his arm. At the clinic, Angus lies, to shield Hunham from fault. Afterward, at a café, Hunham rescues Angus from an argument with a crippled war veteran.

On Christmas Eve, Angus, Hunham, Mary, and Barton's janitor, Danny, go to a party held by the school office overseer, Lydia Crane. While Angus plays with Lydia's niece over finger painting, Hunham is frustrated to find Lydia has a huge other, and an intoxicated Mary separates over her child's demise. Hunham demands leaving ahead of schedule, in spite of fights from Angus, who irately exclaims that his dad is dead, and Mary chastens Hunham for his heartlessness.

Hunham assembles a little Christmas festivity, and with Mary's influence, he concedes Angus' desire for a "field trip" to Boston. Dropping Mary off in Roxbury to invest energy with her pregnant sister, Angus and Hunham bond over different exercises in Boston, including ice skating and a visit to the Gallery of Expressive arts, Boston.

They find a colleague from Hunham's Harvard College days, presently a fruitful scholar, provoking Hunham to lie about his own vocation, as Angus cooperates. Hunham uncovers to Angus that he was ousted from Harvard, in the wake of being outlined for counterfeiting by the child of an inheritance benefactor, which destroyed his profession prospects and constrained him to get back to Barton, as an educator.

While getting a film at the Orpheum Theater, Angus slips away, however he is immediately gotten and makes sense that his dad is really alive, bound at a close by sanatorium. Hunham takes Angus to see his dad, whose dysfunctional behavior divided his family, and consoles Angus that he can turn into his own man. The two join Mary and Danny to observe New Year's Eve by watching the Times Square Ball drop on television and lighting a M-80 firecracker in the school kitchen.

At the point when school resumes, after special times of year, Angus' mom and stepfather show up at Barton. Hunham is gathered at the superintendent's office. It is uncovered that Angus' visit to his dad was against his mom's desires and that he gave his dad a snow globe, taken from Lydia's party, driving his dad to have a fierce episode. This is the straw that broke the camel's back for Angus' mom and his stepfather, who are ready to send him to military school. Hunham goes to bat for Angus and assumes the fault for the excursion. He is terminated, yet Angus is permitted to remain at Barton.

Mary, who has come to better terms with the death of her child, gives Hunham a scratch pad for the monograph he has long needed to compose. He and Angus share a sincere farewell. Leaving the school, Hunham drinks the expensive cognac he stole from the headmaster before spitting it out and driving away from the school.

CAST

- Paul Giamatti as Paul Hunham, a classics teacher at the Barton Academy boarding school
- Dominic Sessa as Angus Tully, a Barton student left on campus during Christmas break
- Da'Vine Joy Randolph as Mary Lamb, Barton head cook and bereaved mother
- Carrie Preston as Miss Lydia Crane, a Barton faculty member
- Brady Hepner as Teddy Kountze, Angus's enemy; one of five holdovers
- Ian Dolley as Alex Ollerman, the son of Mormon missionaries; one of five holdovers

- Jim Kaplan as Ye-Joon Park, an international student from Korea; one of five holdovers
- Michael Provost as Jason Smith, the Barton football team's quarterback; one of five holdovers
- Andrew Garman as Dr. Hardy Woodrip, the headmaster of Barton Academy
- Naheem Garcia as Danny, a Barton janitor
- Stephen Thorne as Thomas Tully, Angus' institutionalized father
- Gillian Vigman as Judy Clotfelter, Angus' mother
- Tate Donovan as Stanley Clotfelter, Angus' stepfather
- Darby Lily Lee-Stack as Elise, Angus's romantic interest

MUSIC

Mark Orton composed the original music for The Holdovers. It also includes some famous Christmas songs as well as music from The Allman Brothers Band, Tony Orlando and Dawn,

Labi Siffre, Badfinger, Shocking Blue, Damien Jurado, Herb Alpert, Gene Autry, Temptations, Chet Baker, Artie Shaw, and Cat Stevens from the 1970s. Back Lot Music released the soundtrack digitally on November 10, 2023, and on compact disc and vinyl on November 17.

PRODUCTION

The Holdovers is the second coordinated effort between chief Alexander Payne and entertainer Paul Giamatti after Sideways (2004). Payne imagined the film's idea subsequent to watching Marcel Pagnol's 1935 film Merlusse, and reached David Hemingson to compose the screenplay, having perused a TV pilot by Hemingson that was likewise set in a boarding school. In June 2021, Miramax procured the circulation rights. In mid 2022, Da'Vine Euphoria Randolph and Carrie Preston joined the cast. Recording started in Massachusetts on January 27, 2022. Location chief Kai Quinlan, who recently chipped away at other New Britain set films like Spotlight and Dark Mass, drew on her Massachusetts childhood for the film.

For the made up Barton Foundation, five Massachusetts schools were utilized as areas: Groton, Northfield Mount Hermon, Deerfield Foundation, St. Imprint's School and Fairhaven High School. Dominic Sessa, featuring in his most memorable film job as Angus, went to Deerfield in the class of 2022. The film likewise shot at the noteworthy Somerville and Orpheum theaters, and on the Boston Normal. Payne later said that catching the 1970s stylish was somewhat simple since "change comes gradually to New England".

RELEASE

A unique screening of the film was held for purchasers on September 11, 2022. The following day, it was accounted for that Center Highlights had obtained circulation privileges for $30 million. The film was booked for a restricted dramatic delivery on November 10, 2023, followed by wide delivery on November 22.

In any case, it was pushed up to a restricted delivery on October 27, followed by a wide delivery on November 10. It is planned for discharge in the Unified Realm by General Pictures UK on January 19, 2024.

The Holdovers' reality debut was held at the 50th Telluride Film Celebration on August 31, 2023. It likewise screened at the 2023 Toronto Worldwide Film Celebration on September 10, 2023, where it was sprinter up for Individuals' Decision Award. It was additionally welcomed to be displayed in the 28th Busan Global Film Celebration's 'Symbol' area, where it was screened on October 7, 2023.

Profits

The film made $211,093 from six auditoriums in its initial end of the week, a normal of $35,082 per venue. It extended to 64 performance centers in its subsequent end of the week, making $599,833. It then made $3.2 million from 778 venues in its third weekend. Proceeding to grow, it made $2.7 million in both its fourth and fifth weekends.

AN OUTLINE OF THE MOVIE

"The Holdovers" happens in New Britain some place, in 1970, at a all boys boarding school called Barton, where the understudies who can't return home for Christmas end up spending their breaks being taken care of by Paul Hunham (Paul

Giamatti), the sourest, most bombastic educator the film can find.

He shows old human advancements and highly esteems being the kind of principled teacher who fails congresspersons' children and says stuff like, "Such are the changes of life" and "Tune in, you hormonal vulgarian!" He has a bad odor and speaks Greek and Latin out of spite as well as goodwill. Except for the room, the man can read everything.

In reasonableness, the children are difficult, by the same token. They put out little snares for Hunham's haughtiness and sic their daddies on the chairmen, who then, at that point, overwhelm him. Absolutely, the glass eye he utilizes has made him simply more risible to them. Presently he is right here, as stuck as the five castoffs he's compelled to direct.

Furthermore, the moment maybe the film's set to be a deft private academy escapade that sets wily rascals in opposition to a lemony smarty pants, it presents a shock. It's an elegant, laugh uncontrollably Christmas supernatural occurrence that whisks away four of the young men toward the finish of the main demonstration. Be that as it may, one of them, a practically cool lone kid named Angus Tully (Dominic Sessa), can't go on the grounds that no one can arrive at his folks. (He was prepared to relax on St. Kitts, yet his mom takes off without him.)

THE REVIEW

The Extras, essayist chief Alexander Payne's startlingly great new film, is a wonderful occasion seeing as you're yearning for the sort of film that used to be plentiful and is currently unfortunately scant. It's a warm, discerning parody show that causes you to feel associated with your kindred individuals. It appears to be peculiar in any event, composing that expression, presently something like this of the past with regards to Hollywood.

Also, Payne is aware of how past it is in this affectionately acknowledged period piece, set in the weeks paving the way to and traversing Christmas through New Year's 1970. Enchantingly acknowledged in everything about, the film addresses the made up Barton Foundation, a customary old WASP private academy outside Boston, Massachusetts, so as to help you to remember social qualities that are both not really well beyond, but simultaneously "as long gone." That is the manner by which works of art educator and old history buff Paul

Hunham (Paul Giamatti) would put it, just to get a normally discourteous and uncomprehending reaction from one of his young understudies: " As dead as the what?" "A Barton man never lies," is one of the clichés presented by Hunham, who can't satisfy the standard anything else than his understudies can. In any case, it's touching to think there was ever a culture that put resources into the conviction that it could shape residents in such unimaginably temperate ways.

Payne took the reason for the movie from a much prior period — a 1935 French movie called Merlusse, composed and coordinated by Marcel Pagnol, who was noted for his warm humanist film. That film likewise includes a testy, severe, profoundly despised instructor who gets stuck disapproving of a little gathering of understudies during the Christmas occasions. Simply pursuing that sentence lets you know the fundamental plot of both Merlusse and The Extras — educators and understudies will find different aspects to one another's characters throughout the span of half a month of segregated harmony, and security in groundbreaking, extraordinary ways.

So no large amazements there. In any case, Payne tracks down numerous ways of presenting more modest amazements throughout seeking after that expansive wistful account. In fact, there are so many that the entire film takes on a bracing newness that is delightfully at odds with how consciously it is rooted in the past.

It specifically interfaces the historical backdrop of Western human advancement, America, New Britain, and world class private academies, with the individual parts of every one of the principal characters. The stuffy, pipe-smoking Hunham tells his dissatisfied student, "You have to look at

the past if you want to understand the present."
This is while they're remaining in the
unsurprisingly void old history part of a Boston
gallery.

Naturally, Payne is also evoking the past of
filmmaking; he has stated in interviews that his
objective was not only to evoke films from the
early 1970s but also to come as close as possible
to making one today.

Payne says that it is still possible to find places in
New England that look the same as they did fifty
years ago, or even one hundred and fifty years
ago, if necessary. Furthermore he carries
incredible aversion to the muffled tans and blues
of the variety conspire, as well as the subtleties of
attire, furniture, and music. Indeed, even the
period-explicit vehicles are superbly utilized and
messy.

The film continuously centers around three characters, a particularly improbable triplet. Hunham — as despised by the vast majority of the workforce and the dignitary as he is by the students — is one of those neglected know-it-alls who's worked for such a long time at one school, showing similar classes, they appear part of the actual structure.

Giamatti, rejoined with Payne interestingly since their enormous 2004 satire hit Sideways, is breathtaking in a section Payne composed explicitly for him. He succeeds at sensationalizing actual grossness and distress — simply see his star-production execution as unkempt, disease stricken Harvey Pekar in American Magnificence (1999) for confirmation. Notwithstanding his curmudgeonly character and exclusive interests, Hunham likewise experiences a glandular condition that makes him smell like a fish.

Giamatti's so persuasive in the job, individuals who've seen The Holdovers are as of now inquiring as to whether he truly has a glass eye or experiences exotropia (the outward turning of one eye) like the person does. Hunham's angry understudies refer to him as "Walleye," in addition to other things, and there's hypothesis about which eye one ought to take a gander at in discussion, which Paul — consistently cryptic and looking for the explanatory benefit — distinctively will not uncover.

Hunham's more established teen student Angus Tully (played by Dominic Sessa in a momentous film debut) appears at first to be simply one more evil, jeering rich youngster, however he's more brilliant than the larger part. He gets the best test grade in class just before special times of year, a B+. (Most likely hardass Hunham never gives As in that fearless old world before grade expansion.)

In any case, Angus is a whimpering, whining, pestering jerk very much like a large portion of his companions until he out of nowhere figures out he's not going on the normal opulent occasion to St Kitts in the West Indies with his mom and new stepfather. All things considered, they've chosen to go on a late special night outing and abandon him for these special seasons.

The third fundamental person is Mary Sheep (Da'Vine Happiness Randolph, likewise giving a gigantic execution), who runs the school cafeteria and has experienced a new languishing loss, the passing of her teen child Curtis, killed in the Vietnam War. She spends the holidays at the academy because, as she puts it, "it's the last place I was with him."

We see an enormous photograph of Curtis Sheep in the extravagantly old world Protestant church at Barton Foundation, where there's little recognition for him as a feature of the last administrations before special times of year. Curtis is dark, and wearing his tactical uniform in the photograph. However he and his mom aren't the main minorities at the institute — one of the five "extras" is pitiably pining to go home to Korean, Ye Joon Park (Jim Kaplan) — there's an inundating ocean of white countenances around them.

At last we discover that Curtis was permitted to go to Barton Foundation on a grant since his mom worked there, and after graduation, he'd joined the help to pay for school on the GI Bill.

Hunham is delicate to Mary's despondency at a school taking care of the well off, where, as he tells Angus harshly, understudies don't end up serving in Vietnam.

"But Curtis Sheep," says Angus.

"Truth be told, aside from Curtis Sheep," says Hunham viciously. Paul's own disdain for his understudies depends on a disenthralled class hatred and an obliterated scholarly vocation, which is bit by bit uncovered as he comes to trade confidences with Angus that get perpetually commonly uncovering and, as Paul puts it, rigorously "entre nous."

Everything works so well. How could it be this good? Certainly it'll sink into rank nostalgic sentimentalism. Or on the other hand there will be frail exhibitions. Or on the other hand the consummation will get bungled. But no. Each exhibition is brilliant, in any event, when the person is an especially extreme one to play. For instance, Miss Lydia Crane is a Barton employee who is uncommonly pleasant to Paul — she's one of those extraordinarily sweet ladies that you nearly can't completely accept that exist, however you've likely met one in your life, and Carrie Preston makes her so adorable it harms.

In addition, Stephen Thorne plays Thomas Tully, Angus's father, who is severely mentally ill and in an institutional setting. It is harrowing to watch his eyes dart around in an uncertain manner.

The general tone of the film is perfectly tweaked. And, surprisingly, the completion, which is both dismal and confident simultaneously, is dealt with perfectly. Alexander Payne has been blamed for peering down on his characters in films like "Political decision," "Resident Ruth," and "Nebraska." This analysis is a little shallow, however reasonable, given the silly characters ruling those movies and the line between finding individuals engaging and deriding them. This is brought up on the grounds that his most recent, "The Remnants," contains not a scintilla of this component of his vocation. He, on the other hand, adores these people. It shows up in every frame, line delivery, and plot decision. What's more, during a time of expanding pessimism. Many individuals will cherish them as well.

Payne returns from the sad "Scaling down" by rejoining with the star of seemingly his most cherished film, "Sideways." Paul Giamatti gets his most extravagant part in years as Paul Hunham, a severe teacher at the lofty Barton Foundation in the mid '70s. (In his opening monologue, Payne jokingly stated that since he had spent his entire career essentially producing comedies set in the 1970s, he figured he would finally direct a film at that time.) Hunham is by and large despised by understudies and staff, albeit a partner named Lydia (Carrie Preston) makes the crotchety elderly person Christmas treats. During the Christmas break, Hunham is yelling at students for the smallest of infractions when he isn't handing out failing grades and assignments. He's one of those folks who doesn't have a lot of force in his life, so he utilizes it combatively, leaving him few companions.

Seven Things You Need to Know About "Dracula" by Bram Stoker Every holiday break, a few kids have to stay over instead of going home. This forces a lonely man like Paul to watch over them, even giving them homework because that's really all he knows how to do.

Paul, a student named Angus (Dominic Sessa in a breakout role), and the head cook Mary (Da'Vine Joy Randolph) are all that remain from this break after a series of events. They're three individuals at exceptionally particular section breaks in their lives, yet they will impact each other in an endearing and certified manner. The play written by David Hemingson is about those wonderful turns in our lives when a stranger can lead us in a new direction we hadn't thought of, and how they can happen long after we think we've adjusted enough. It has some irrefutable buzzwords, yet Payne and his group figure out how to make the existence examples natural, declining to construct their dramedy on unsurprising unexpected developments. All things considered, this one is about the flightiness of life.

In the event that Hunham is the hesitant mentor of this triplet, Mary is the mother, a pain stricken lady who has recently lost her child in the Vietnam War. Randolph is downplayed and moving, tracking down the heaviness of distress. She just seems to have a harder time getting around the world. I can't envision the aggravation of losing a youngster, yet I accept it would make a great deal of days like a sand trap. On the opposite side of the table, Angus is a 15-year-old with a razor mind yet the sort of hostility that accompanies vulnerability. His folks don't need him over special times of year. He doesn't know where he pursues Barton. Vietnam might be the destination. To say that he connects with Hunham for direction would be an embellishment, however these two introductory foes begin to comprehend each other. Through the friendship of a young man who is pondering where he is going, Hunham begins to examine how he got here.

All of this doesn't catch how predictably amusing "The Holdovers" is from start to finish. In the early scenes, Payne uses Giamatti's irascibility in hilarious ways that make it stronger when those walls start to fall. Although Randolph doesn't get many laughs, he can always nail a punchline. Sessa is the real star of this movie; she starts out a little bland but grows with the film. This is one of those acting turns wherein it seems like you're watching a future star. He has the energy of both a main man and an idiosyncratic person entertainer simultaneously. You know, how it felt with '70s comedies when appeal and appeal were vital, and mannerism wasn't a wrongdoing. Sessa would have been a star then. He will be one at this point.

Hollywood has a long history of accounts of "stopgap families that learn something," however at that point for what reason does "The Leftovers" feel so new? It's presumably in light of the fact that it's been for such a long time since one of these accounts felt this valid. Payne and his group perceive the adages of this life illustration, however they implant them with insights that will continuously be immortal. Everybody has that startling kinship or even mentorship with somebody who everlastingly changed their heading throughout everyday life. Also, everybody has that youngster who has stunned them out of their balance, either through uncovering what they have become or neglected to be.

The movie "The Holdovers" is always smart and funny about people who are easy to root for and are like people we know. It is not its greatest achievement to be able to see yourself in Paul, Angus, or Mary. It's that you will win each of the three.

Printed in Great Britain
by Amazon

38930250R00020